Corazón

From mine to yours

Saniya Attar

BookLeaf Publishing
India | USA | UK

Made with ❤ on the BookLeaf Publishing Platform
www.bookleafpub.in
www.bookleafpub.com

Dedication

This book belongs to anyone, who has ever been told that they will always be too much...

Preface

There are parts of me scattered in this book. Some old and most of them very old. But its all about remembering the roots and what led you there.

Acknowledgements

Grateful to everyone who has inspired a light in me and also the people who could only bring the absence of it.

1. You

You..
The spots on moon
The sand on the beach
The unlit candle
The stained page of my favorite book
The smeared ink of my diary page
The broken feather of a bird
The tear confounded to my eyes
The relentless hope
The aching heart
The lost soul
You..
Not perfect.
Yet the beauty of everything..

2. Falling

So when I thought about love
It was always someone with colored eyes
Mind of an Einstein
Obviously very romantic.
The usual.
Because every girl thinks these are the necessities for an eligible, decent guy amiright?
We think we deserve the best
Even when we ourselves are nowhere close to it.
But love came so unimaginable, opposite!
Love was weird
Almost felt like he did not want to be heard.
He was awkward and reserved
He enjoyed sarcasm though, I observed
Love had a great taste in music!
And his touch felt so therapeutic

Wait! that was a desperate attempt to rhyme

His touch really was infact magic
But love had a patchy beard
Did hair just give up on him? I feared.
Love snored like a truck
My sleep ran out of all it's luck

But love had the most beautiful voice when he sang
Literally made my heart walls bang!
Love made the best food
I felt my soul had travelled all this while for it, t'was that good.
Now this is embarrassing,
But love ate his ice cream with milk!
Said "Mmm it feels like silk!"
And love fought over the smallest things
Like "Do you know how much mess your shopping brings?"
But love made sure to buy me Chipotle when I was upset.
And kept keys in my bag that I always forget.
Love made me feel beautiful everyday
Even if I wore sweatpants and mismatched socks on a weekday.
Love made me realize..
Colored eyes deceive too.
Einstein is dead.
And romance is well, all around, you just need to find it.

3. Once

I am in love with someone else but I missed you today..
I missed you because I needed to be reminded of what it took me to get here.
I missed you because I had to inhale everything around me that was changing..
I missed you because I needed to be reminded why some people in love like we we were, still don't make it..
I missed you because I finally slept peacefully one night, and I realized how many years had passed since you weren't a reason behind it
A part of me will always love you
And that is the part about myself I dislike the most
I changed careers
I moved places
I fell in love, again.
And still. The fact that I can so distinctly remember your smile and the way it curved even though rest of your face is now a blur to me..is why I missed you.
I knew I had to learn the way you had with words is why I missed you.
I have learned. I have grown. And I will find an year where I won't miss you anymore.

4. Me?

Would you think about me?
When you look in the mirror and see you don't look the same as you did when you met me..
When the windows around our favorite café
through which you used to smile at me from just across the road, are now tinted..
When the pothole on the road to your home, driving trying to avoid it,
I used to purposely lean a little on your shoulder, is now repaired..
When the shore of the lake, where you first said those three words,
now stands a house with wooden fence around it..
When you are just standing lost in your thoughts and no one is there to hold you from behind and just press their cheek into your back anymore..
When you kiss someone else's mouth and realize their lips don't feel the same,
they don't feel like you are home even when you are away from it..
So tell me, would you think about me?

5. Foreign

I have immigrant in my veins
I have roof of my first home burnt in me
I have laughs of my childhood flowing through.
That water, that warm sun, that sand,
Are the condiments I carry with me
My language is foreign
So is my skin
But we hold the same longing in our eyes
Tell me, how are we different?
When you meet me you'll see..
I'll melt into you and you'll melt into me.

6. This letter is for my mother.

My mother does this thing you know,
She would say a straight no to anything I would ask
And hours later would come by to confirm if what I actually asked for is absolutely needed and would try to reason with me..

I would come back home from a tiring day and she would keep tea and my favorite snack ready for me no matter how tired she has been after taking care of the house all day.

I remember my sister used to come back so late at night from her rotations, and no matter what time, my mother would wake up to atleast wish her good night and ask her if anything is needed.

I have felt guilty for brushing her off so many times when I was in a bad mood or had a long day, I used to forget that my mother had been home alone the entire day and all she wanted was few minutes with her beloved.

She stood by my father at every step of the way..no

matter how long and hard the fight, she always whispered in his ear to stay strong and always believe in the truth.

She would offer Namaaz on days we were happy or sad or busy or preoccupied and never has she wished anything for herself, and I know everyone thinks its true for their mothers as well, and everyone is right.

I have seen her glow with joy over a smallest pair of earrings that she would like and the shine of brightest diamond wouldn't be close to it.

She has openly cried in our happiness and sadness but never let her smile fade even when she lost her father to terminal illness..

She stays 8,431 miles away for 12 months from her daughters and still somehow raised us to be the women we are today. And if there is one saying I have absolute proof of is 'God couldn't be everywhere so he made mother.

7. Story

Wait!
Turn around.
Look at me..
You haven't finished your wine yet,
There are still stains of our last night on the table
And you haven't pulled the curtains yet
There is still darkness for our souls lurking in between.
And and..you haven't rinsed your mouth yet,
The filth you said hasn't washed away with apologies..
And you haven't held me and stared into my eyes yet,
You haven't seen the passion I had for you, leave.
So wait!
Please.
I want you to be here when the skeleton of our love has
no stories to tell anymore..

8. Hide

I close my eyes,
dark to find my own galaxies
constellations of my pieces
going through every love I find.
This figure unseen
And the depth unfound.
No orion in sight,
convolution of my own smithereens
What would I name a universe,
with all its stars waiting to be endowed.
within burning
there is my sun,
mind, heart, soul, pulled into you
but not enough to burn in the pyre.
Eons have passed
as I make the triplet complete a revolution
interrupted by dilemmas
misguided by storms
separated by longing
Kept together in belief.
I turn red and blue and green
The next explosion in making.
Mad scientists in fury,
I wait for Galileo to find me.

9. Dream

I will follow you through dreams
And look in your shadow
And I will decipher every thought of yours

Every move you make
Every finger you lift to talk
I will consume your evil
And hold your hand across the dirt

I will fill your emptiness
With my colors
Make you abstract
Only this artist will understand the art that you are.

Your earth will blossom
And I will make your moon, be the sun.
I will bring stars home
And I will make you fly on my broken wings

I will love you now.

10. Warm

Go.
Leave again.
People will always be like seasons..
Look you in the eye,
Touch your skin
Make you memorize their pattern
And then change.
So be a maze within yourself
Try to find a path of you that hasn't been seen..
A voice of you that can't speak.
Be your own sky
With your own rain and fire
Because honey, you will change too
Atleast you will have sun within yourself when the world turns cold..

11. Beat

Shhh!
You are hurting my ears
You have already bruised my wrists
Snap.
I heard that stick break
Atleast its not my spine yet
Wait.
I'll get you your water
Maybe it will drench my throat
Rub.
Don't hug me.
I can't anticipate when one of your hands
Is going pull my hair.
Please don't kiss me.
Your lips hurt now
I don't know if you could hurt my tongue too
Drag.
I will dress for you again tonight
Maybe you will stop if I look too nice...
I will move in all your favorite ways
I will kiss my respect goodbye. Again.
It waits for me to run away with it at the door.
Tonight I might run.

12. King

I'll pretend its all good
That your hands are not making
My upbringing a crime
That they are burning a million hearts
That they are not threatening my beliefs
I'll pretend its all good
When your promises are drowning like
the sculptures you submerge each year, after worship.
People meant to protect, now only worry about the foot
thats stomping them
I'll pretend its all good
When an entire country now feels homeless.
Kids you claim our 'future' are now lying on beds with
sutures.
But now answer.
What will you control when the eyes you think
are so filled with love ,
Will turn red in mutiny against you..
When your own throne is on fire
And you won't know what winning feels like
You are bulldozing on relations
That weren't nurtured by you in the first place
So who gave you the right claiming a motherland
And then abusing its care..

Remember,
We are not ruled, we are the rulers
And a rebellion even makes walls crumble.

13. Flow

I wish I was the blood flowing in my veins
I would rise to my eyes everytime you would call my name
I would drop to my feet at every heartbreak
I would clot at the thought of you leaving tonight
Splash I would go to my heart
Racing
Because you are holding me so close, its the same air we breathe
I would want to be set free when I leap
Stay still when I am happy
I would be on surface, with our bodies so close
Because even if blood,
I would want to be met with yours.

14. Journey

There is a girl trying to sleep tonight
All tucked in
As warm as summer
but her mind keeps running
tip toeing around subconsciously
She keeps hearing the sounds outside
nothing enough to make her open her eyes
but enough to not let her breathe evenly
she stumbles across regrets
That door is for nights when more alcohol goes through veins
she paddles to secrets now
those are for times when she feels brave enough
tonight she can afford to be scared
Lies, dishonesty, betrayals
she entered the quick sand
better to stand still before they swallow her whole
Pffft! That was close, anymore and she won't have made it alive
Hurt and love
she is surprised they were together, again
didn't the process of let go complete?
she knows she needs to step back
more and more and more

Sounds are getting louder
lungs get heavier
toes curl in haste
there it is, she sees it now
the happy,
times, memories and people
and you still stood out like a rose in this dead forest
she doesn't seem to get away anymore
and she finally rests
but morning,
there is more distance now when she opens her eyes again
maybe someday another road of mind gets me closer to feel you again.

15. Burden

I walk on these snow laden paths
Sometimes with nowhere to go
And look up to the trees
Hanging, as the white ash weighs them down
Don't let it fall with quivers
Don't let it sway with the threatening wind
Just keep hugging it.
Its almost as if they know someone's constantly watching
And if they let the ice go, no one would want to see the brown skeleton anymore,
They won't be as beautiful
As mesmerizing,
Mortals like us
Living like us
And what a pity, to perhaps know they could think like us..
Maybe thats where it starts
From roots to branches to us
Everybody bearing their scars
And everybody to damn scared to show..

16. Lifetime

I will tell you one day
Of the things I did and the songs I play
Great many people I met
Some stayed and some fell off the net
But I still won't be able to tell
Of how much love I ever felt
The dreams I had
The fantasies I planned
Because then I would have to think of you
And I never only want to think of you
I want you.
I want you in flesh and blood and skin
And I want you to feel my bones and veins and skin
And I want you in this damned lifetime
And all next damned lifetimes
And if there are none,
Then I want to cut this time in pieces
And give you every last one of those pieces
But even that won't be enough
Because lovers as us weren't made just so we could be together
Lovers as us were made to be sung forever
To be remembered
And by children recollected,

We are meant to be melted in each others eyes
And be announced by each others smiles
We are to be danced across and empty ballroom
And I want to be lost in you waltzing across an empty ballroom
We are to be written about till inks fade
We are rare, love, like jade
So think when I can't say what my heart screams
I will always stay yours in all your dreams.

17. Rest

There will be burials
of the moments we had
and time would come to pay its respect
And I would be there to see you
one last time.
Notice how your hair follows the wind
and your eyes burn with the light
how there is not a curve formed by your lips
And how your gaze never met mine.
But I would hope you look
At the ruins we have carved
See if the bones of your faults
Found peace with apologies
Because I made this pyre
With wood cut out of every wound you gave
But left no blood of blame
So its neat and arranged
Look closely now.
Watch how the smoke of past
Never bothers your heart.
I won't show you,
I will be lighting the fire this time.

18. Color

I have painted a picture
A riot one at that.
Stands on easel of my mind
Red would be the color of first love
And blue would be the end of it.
I will fill in sadness with white.
Because even on my darkest days,
I choose to shine bright.
Dappled black,
My demons only have slight shadows
Neon unspoken words
Screaming for attention,
Amber my center still lit for you.
Rose pleasures for lonelier rotations
I would shape in a face of mine
You have never seen before
Yet keep nuances
To warm you.
There will be a world
Where my art yearns to be sold to you.

19. Moon

Chaand kehte the mujhe
maine roop bhi kuch waise dikhaye
Kabhi chupkar
Kabhi sare aam
Kabhi adhure
Par khwaab sabko dikhaaye
Mujhe dhundne aate hai log
durr durr se
Jaise chaand ka tasavur kiya hai
waisi na dikhun toh maayus hokar chale jaate hai
Par yeh bhul jaate hai
Ki chaand par bhi toh daag hote hai.
Aasmaan par uss chaand ka har nuks qubool
Uski har chaanv
uska har husn pyaara
Zameen ke ird gird ghumkar
jaane kya dhundta hai..
shayad ek pyaar hai inka
Na mil sakte hai na juda ho sakte hai
Kuch pal saath akele bitaane ke liye
shayad chaand humse chupta hai
Roz kuch iss pani se
Apni shayari padhta hai
Roz kuch yeh nadi thoda aur muskuraati hai

Minaron par chaandni barsaata hai
aur kuch kabrein bhi zinda ho uthti hai
Pattiyon se channkar jo
musafir ko bhi rasta dikhlaaye
Waise chaand ke jalwe par toh sab haar jaaye
shayad isiliye,
Chaand kehte the mujhe
kyunki maine roop bhi kuch waise dikhaye

20. Freeze

I get closer each day to undo the current me
No side of this cassette comes without static
I sit on that same couch everyday
Staring at a different show everyday
My mind runs the things I could be doing in that time
And energy runs the things I am doing at that time
Unhinged are my desires and ambitions
Clogged are my arteries of procrastination
Chaotic thoughts about past lovers
They did not deserve me but they still hover
Not in my phone but in my constant rotor
In this chosen path to be alone
There comes peace with all of its enemies
"Oh! Look how casually she leans on his shoulder
And look how deeply he kisses her"
There is that drop of lemon jealousy
Hidden in crossed fingers that maybe
someday that would be me.
I lie in my bed free to spread around like cheese
Wishing there was someone stealing this blanket from me
But enough about that,
Redundancy bores me.
I am constantly looking for the next skill to be Jack at

And I am a Master at daydreaming once its found
I have a book next to my bed
With the same marked page from a month,
just waiting to be read
This summer I want to learn how to ride a bike
And maybe just take the travelled path for the hike
The places I want to see
The skies I want to mindlessly gaze
The suns I want to watch disappear in a haze
The moons and stars I can't foresee
Every inch of this universe slowly becoming me
As I unbecome what was the yesterday of me..

21. Hope

There is love that people write about
How they fell in it
How they felt in it
When their skin could not tell the difference
between a morning and a goodnight kiss
When the grave of their scars,
Grew roses of tomorrow
When everyday they wondered
Gosh! Was I even alive before this human!
When there was wine and dine
but also bickering and compromises
When each day that they came home,
they could smell them in every curtain fold
When they could just watch them asleep
and try to sync their breathing
When they reached for a bowl
and out of habit just grabbed two
When every hair strand they found
made them felt the relief of them being around
When they moved a certain way
it would indicate a time to put their arm around
When they sang their favorite song
and all they had to do was hum the tune
When they felt the world collapsing with both its arms

and all they had to do was look into each others eyes
How they fell in them
How they felt in them
There was love that people wrote about.

www.ingramcontent.com/pod-product-compliance
Lightning Source LLC
Chambersburg PA
CBHW051750130826
49812CB00033B/1081
9789370928107